LITTLE BIGHORN BATTLEFIELD NATIONAL MONUMENT

By Marie Roesser

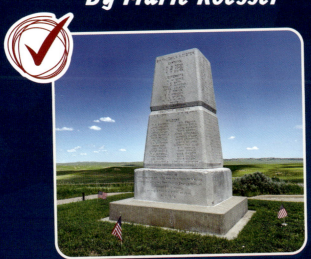

Enslow PUBLISHING

Please visit our website, www.enslow.com. For a free color catalog of all our high-quality books, call toll free 1-800-398-2504 or fax 1-877-980-4454.

Library of Congress Cataloging-in-Publication Data
Names: Roesser, Marie, author.
Title: Little Bighorn Battlefield National Monument / Marie Roesser.
Description: Buffalo : Enslow Publishing, 2026. | Series: America's amazing landmarks | Includes index.
Identifiers: LCCN 2024052208 (print) | LCCN 2024052209 (ebook) | ISBN 9781978543928 (library binding) | ISBN 9781978543911 (paperback) | ISBN 9781978543935 (ebook)
Subjects: LCSH: Little Bighorn Battlefield National Monument (Mont.)–Juvenile literature. | CYAC: Little Bighorn, Battle of the, Mont., 1876–Juvenile literature.
Classification: LCC E83.876 .R67 2026 (print) | LCC E83.876 (ebook) | DDC 973.8/2–dc23/eng/20241216
LC record available at https://lccn.loc.gov/2024052208
LC ebook record available at https://lccn.loc.gov/2024052209

Published in 2026 by
Enslow Publishing
2544 Clinton Street
Buffalo, NY 14224

Copyright © 2026 Enslow Publishing

Cover Designer: **Nicholas Switalski**
Interior Designer: Rachel Rising
Editor: Therese Shea

Photo credits: Cover, SveKo/Shutterstock.com; pp. 1, 3-24 Jeffery Edwards/Shutterstock.com; pp. 1, 5, 7, 11, 15, 17, 19, 21 Oleksandr Poliashenko/Shutterstock.com; p. 5 Steve Boice/Shutterstock.com; p. 5 (map) Sunflowerr/Shutterstock.com; p. 7 https://en.m.wikipedia.org/wiki/File:Funeral_scaffold_of_a_Sioux_chief_0044v_crop.jpg; pp. 8,11 Everett Collection/Shutterstock.com; p. 9 Wirestock Creators/Shutterstock.com; p. 13 https://commons.wikimedia.org/wiki/File:GenGACuster.jpg; p. 15 Andrea Izzotti/Shutterstock.com; p. 16 Aaron J Hill/Shutterstock.com; p. 17 Breck P. Kent/Shutterstock.com; p. 19 Takeshi Bennett/Shutterstock.com; p. 21 Zack Frank/Shutterstock.com.

All rights reserved.
No part of this book may be reproduced in any form without permission in writing from the publisher, except by a reviewer.

Printed in the United States of America

Some of the images in this book illustrate individuals who are models. The depictions do not imply actual situations or events.

CPSIA compliance information: Batch #CSENS26: For further information contact Enslow Publishing, at 1-800-398-2504.

CONTENTS

AN IMPORTANT PLACE............4

BEFORE THE BATTLE..............6

THE BATTLE 12

REMEMBER AND RESPECT 16

VISIT THE MONUMENT 20

GLOSSARY 22

FOR MORE INFORMATION 23

INDEX 24

BOLDFACE WORDS APPEAR IN THE GLOSSARY.

AN IMPORTANT PLACE

In 1876, Little Bighorn Valley was the **site** of a battle between the U.S. Army and Native Americans. Today, the Little Bighorn Battlefield National Monument helps us remember what happened. A national monument is a place set aside and cared for by the government because it's important to the nation.

LITTLE BIGHORN BATTLEFIELD NATIONAL MONUMENT IS IN SOUTHEASTERN MONTANA.

BEFORE THE BATTLE

In 1868, the U.S. government made a treaty, or agreement, with Sioux (SOO) and Arapaho peoples. The treaty created the Great Sioux **Reservation**. It also set aside the Black Hills of Wyoming and South Dakota for Native Americans. These mountains were **sacred** to many Native peoples.

Sioux, around 1834

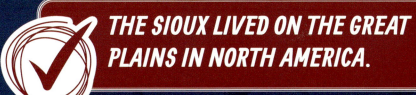

THE SIOUX LIVED ON THE GREAT PLAINS IN NORTH AMERICA.

In 1874, gold was found in the Black Hills. White miners began to settle there. Native Americans asked the government to remove the settlers, but the government wouldn't. The government wanted to buy the Black Hills instead. The Native Americans wouldn't sell their sacred land.

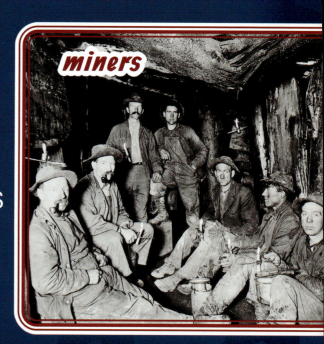

miners

The U.S. government ordered the Native Americans to move onto their reservations. Lakota Sioux, Northern Cheyenne, and Arapaho peoples refused. They were hunters and didn't want to change their ways of life. They were led by Lakota Chief Sitting Bull.

CHIEF SITTING BULL WAS A MEMBER OF THE HUNKPAPA LAKOTA.

THE BATTLE

In spring 1876, U.S. Army soldiers were ordered to force Native Americans onto reservations. On June 25, a group of soldiers led by George Armstrong Custer found Sitting Bull's village in Little Bighorn Valley. **Warriors** saw them coming, so Custer decided to attack right away.

Lieutenant Colonel George Armstrong Custer

Custer and all 210 U.S. soldiers he led were killed during the battle. About 50 Native Americans died too. The Native Americans had won. However, thousands more U.S. soldiers were sent to the area. Finally, the Native Americans were forced to **surrender** and live on reservations.

 THIS IS A CHEYENNE DEERSKIN PAINTING FROM AROUND 1878 OF THE BATTLE OF THE LITTLE BIGHORN.

REMEMBER AND RESPECT

In 1879, the Little Bighorn Battlefield was named a national **cemetery**. In 1881, the U.S. government built a stone **memorial** on a hill where about 45 soldiers, including Custer, had been killed. In 1890, white markers were set up to honor the dead soldiers.

 **THE 7TH U.S. CAVALRY MEMORIAL IS LOCATED ON LAST STAND HILL.**

For many years, Native Americans asked for a memorial at the Little Bighorn site. In 1991, the U.S. government agreed. In 2003, the memorial was finished. It shows three Native warriors riding away as a woman gives one a **shield**.

 THE INDIAN MEMORIAL AT LITTLE BIGHORN BATTLEFIELD NATIONAL MONUMENT IS CALLED "PEACE THROUGH UNITY."

VISIT THE MONUMENT

At Little Bighorn Battlefield National Monument, visitors learn about the battle and its long-reaching effects. They learn about the real-life people on both sides. They are reminded of the importance of different peoples working together toward peace and understanding.

 **LITTLE BIGHORN BATTLEFIELD NATIONAL MONUMENT IS OPEN TO VISITORS MOST DAYS OF THE YEAR.**

GLOSSARY

cemetery: A place where the dead are buried.

memorial: A place, display, or event to remember someone or something.

reservation: Land set aside by the U.S. government for Native Americans.

sacred: Specially blessed, or holy.

shield: Piece of metal or wood used to guard the body in battle.

site: A place where something important happened.

surrender: To give up.

unity: The state of being in agreement and working together.

warrior: A soldier.

FOR MORE INFORMATION

Books

Marcks, Betty. *The Sioux*. Minneapolis, MN: Bellwether Media, 2024.

Pierce, Simon. *Sitting Bull*. Buffalo, NY: Cavendish Square Publishing, 2025.

Websites

Battle of the Little Bighorn
www.ducksters.com/history/native_americans/battle_of_little_big_horn.php
Read more about this famous battle.

Little Bighorn Battlefield National Monument
www.nps.gov/libi/index.htm
Learn about the monument and how to visit it on this National Park Service site.

Publisher's note to educators and parents: Our editors have carefully reviewed these websites to ensure that they are suitable for students. Many websites change frequently, however, and we cannot guarantee that a site's future contents will continue to meet our high standards of quality and educational value. Be advised that students should be closely supervised whenever they access the internet.

INDEX

Arapaho, 6, 10
Black Hills, 6, 8
Cheyenne, 10, 15
Custer, George Armstrong, 12, 14, 16
Lakota, 10, 11
Little Bighorn Valley, 4, 12
memorials, 16, 17, 18, 19
miners, 8
Montana, 5
Sioux, 6, 10
Sitting Bull, 10, 11, 12
treaty, 6
U.S. Army, 4, 12, 14, 16
U.S. government, 10, 16, 18
visitors, 20, 21